nickelodeon™

降世神通

AVATAR

THE LAST AIRBENDER™

Created by
Bryan Konietzko
Michael Dante DiMartino

GURI HIRU

nickelodeon™

降世神通

AVATAR

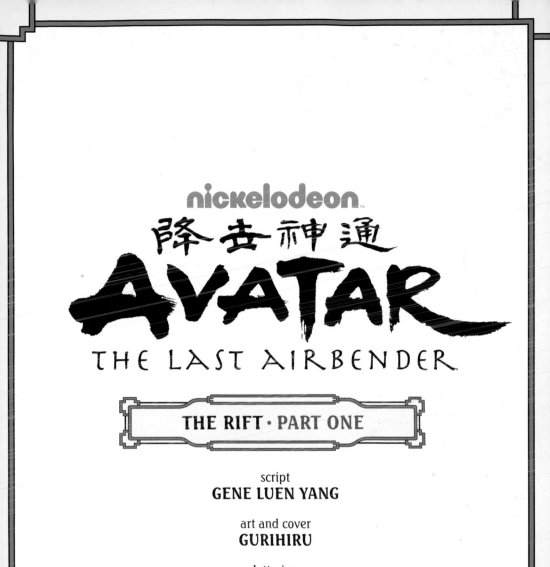

THE LAST AIRBENDER™

script
GENE LUEN YANG

art and cover
GURIHIRU

lettering
MICHAEL HEISLER

DARK HORSE BOOKS

president and publisher
MIKE RICHARDSON

collection designer
JUSTIN COUCH

assistant editors
IAN TUCKER and **AARON WALKER**

editor
DAVE MARSHALL

Special thanks to Linda Lee,
Kat van Dam, James Salerno, and Joan Hilty
at Nickelodeon, and to Bryan Konietzko,
Michael Dante DiMartino,
and Cassie Anderson.

Published by
Dark Horse Books
A division of
Dark Horse Comics LLC
10956 SE Main Street
Milwaukie, OR 97222

DarkHorse.com
Nick.com

International Licensing: (503) 905-2315
To find a comic shop in your area, visit comicshoplocator.com

First edition: March 2014
ISBN 978-1-61655-295-4

3 5 7 9 10 8 6 4
Printed in China.

YU DAO.

ZUKO WAS SUCH A BIG PART OF MAKING THIS HAPPEN. TOO BAD HE COULDN'T JOIN US TODAY!

URSA AND HER FAMILY ARE VISITING THE CAPITAL CITY FOR THE FIRST TIME SINCE HER EXILE. FIRE LORD ZUKO NEEDS TO BE THERE TO SUPPORT THEM.

HOW DID YOUR TENURE AS THE INTERIM FIRE LORD GO, IROH?
I HAD MUCH MORE FUN -- AND MORE ***TEA*** -- THAN I HAD EXPECTED! THE ***NATIONAL TEA APPRECIATION DAY*** WAS A ROUSING SUCCESS!
BUT IT ONLY MADE ME MISS MY LITTLE TEASHOP ALL THE MORE.

YOU'LL BE GOING HOME SOON, I HOPE?
OH YES! ATTENDING THIS IS MY LAST BIT OF OFFICIAL BUSINESS! AFTERWARDS, IT'S BACK TO BA SING SE FOR ME!

LOOKS LIKE THEY'RE READY TO MAKE AN ANNOUNCEMENT!

CITIZENS OF YU DAO, THE ELECTION RESULTS ARE IN! PLEASE WELCOME YOUR CITY'S *NEW COALITION GOVERNMENT!*

LATER.
AH, MY FAVORITE PART OF ANY CELEBRATION -- THE BANQUET!

?

HEY, XING YING, IS ONE OF YOUR FRIENDS COMING LATE?
NO. EVERYONE WHO'S SUPPOSED TO BE HERE IS ALREADY HERE.

HM. I'LL BE RIGHT BACK.

EXCUSE ME! SORRY!

EXCUSE ME, PLEASE! I'M TRYING TO GET--!

EESH.

WHOOOOSH!

COMING THROUGH, RIGHT ABOVE YOU!
WHOOOOO!

OOPS! SORRY ABOUT THAT!
HSH!

HEY! ARE YOU AN ACOLYTE? I DON'T KNOW IF WE'VE EVER MET BEFORE --
WHERE ARE YOU GOING?

WAIT UP!

HOP ON MY AIR SCOOTER! I CAN TAKE YOU TO JOIN THE OTHER ACOLYTES --

AVATAR YANGCHEN!
I CAN'T HEAR ANYTHING YOU'RE SAYING!

I DON'T UNDERSTAND--
NO, NO! DON'T GO!

YANGCHEN!

OH MAN, YU DAO'S GOTTA MAKE BRAND NEW GOVERNMENTS MORE OFTEN! MY MOUTH IS SO HAPPY RIGHT NOW!
YEE-LI, YOU'VE GOT TO TRY THE TURTLE-DUCK!
NO, THANK YOU. THE AIR ACOLYTES FOLLOW THE ANCIENT AIR NOMAD PRACTICE OF VEGETARIANISM.

SORRY TO HEAR THAT. YOUR MOUTH IS MISSING OUT ON A WHOLE LOT OF HAPPINESS.
HOW ARE THINGS AT THE ACADEMY, TOPH?
GOOD, I GUESS.

I'VE GOT SO MANY LILY LIVERS -- ER, STUDENTS -- THESE DAYS, I HAD TO MAKE A BUNCH OF EARTH TENTS OUTSIDE THE SCHOOL JUST TO HOUSE 'EM ALL. I WANNA EXPAND THE BUILDING, BUT WE DON'T HAVE THE MONEY.

WHY DON'T YOU CHARGE TUITION? WITH ALL THOSE STUDENTS, YOU'D BE RICHER THAN THE EARTH KING!
THE BEIFONG METALBENDING ACADEMY ISN'T THAT KIND OF SCHOOL. I DON'T WANT IT TO BE A BUSINESS. WE'RE DOING SOMETHING NEW, YOU KNOW? SOMETHING IMPORTANT.

I MEAN, I DIDN'T CHARGE AANG TUITION. I'M NOT ABOUT TO START NOW.
SPEAKING OF AANG, HAS ANYONE SEEN HIM?

NOPE. BUT WHEN YOU FIND HIM, TELL HIM HE'S GOT TO RECONSIDER THAT VEGETARIAN THING. HIS MOUTH WILL THANK HIM!

NOTHING.

AANG? WHAT'RE YOU DOING OUT HERE?

ON THE WAY HERE, I SAW *AVATAR YANGCHEN* IN THE CROWD.
YANGCHEN...?
YEAH. SHE WAS FOUR AVATARS AGO, THE AIRBENDER AVATAR BEFORE ME. SHE WAS TRYING TO TELL ME SOMETHING, BUT I COULDN'T HEAR HER VOICE.

SO YOU'VE BEEN TRYING TO CONTACT HER THROUGH YOUR MEDITATION BEADS.
I CAN'T GET THROUGH FOR SOME REASON.
MEDITATING JUST HASN'T BEEN GOING ALL THAT WELL LATELY.

SWEETIE, I'M SURE IT'S IMPORTANT. BUT IF YOU CAN'T DO ANYTHING ABOUT IT RIGHT NOW, COME INSIDE. CELEBRATIONS LIKE THIS ARE IMPORTANT, TOO.

THAT'S IT!
CELEBRATIONS! OF COURSE!

AIR ACOLYTES, CLEAR YOUR SCHEDULES TOMORROW! WE'RE GOING ON A *FIELD TRIP!*

YAY!

MAN, YOU GUYS ARE GONNA LOVE THIS!
SIGH DOUBT IT.
OH, CHEER UP, SOKKA. I'LL HELP YOU SHOP FOR A NEW PURSE WHEN WE GET BACK.
NOT A PURSE, A BAG!
A MANLY, MANLY BAG. TO CARRY MY MANLY, MANLY THINGS.
WE'LL BE SURE TO FIND ONE THAT MATCHES YOUR MANLY, MANLY BELT.
TODAY'S ONE OF THE HIGHEST HOLIDAYS ON THE AIR NOMAD CALENDAR: YANGCHEN'S FESTIVAL! IT'S ALSO ONE OF THE FUNNEST!
IT HASN'T BEEN CELEBRATED IN OVER A HUNDRED YEARS! AND WITH EVERYTHING THAT'S HAPPENED, IT MIGHT'VE BEEN COMPLETELY LOST TO HISTORY IF YANGCHEN HERSELF HADN'T REMINDED ME LAST NIGHT.
AVATAR AANG, PLEASE TELL US MORE!
WHERE ARE WE GOING?
AND WHAT ARE WE GOING TO DO?
THOSE ACOLYTE KIDS ARE SUPER NICE AND ALL, BUT DON'T THEY SEEM AWFULLY...
EAGER?
YEAH.
WE'RE GOING TO A CLIFF OVERLOOKING THE OCEAN, WHERE THERE'S THIS GIANT STATUE OF A BEAUTIFUL WOMAN! THAT'S WHERE YANGCHEN'S FESTIVAL BEGINS!

"WE'LL GATHER TOGETHER AND BOW FOUR TIMES, AS A SIGN OF RESPECT.

"THEN WE'LL WALK DOWN THE CLIFF TO A SECLUDED MEADOW, PLAYING TRADITIONAL AIR NOMAD MUSIC ALONG THE WAY!"

OH GOOD! I BROUGHT MY CYMBALS!
CLANG!

"WHEN WE GET TO THE MEADOW, WE'LL EAT A CEREMONIAL AIR NOMAD MEAL!"

LET ME GUESS: TOFU, VEGGIES, AND NOT A LOT OF SALT.
YEP!
SPECTACULAR.

"AFTERWARDS, WE CAN VISIT AN ISLAND JUST OFF THE COAST, WHERE MONK GYATSO USED TO TAKE ME AND THE OTHER KIDS TO FLY KITES.
"THE WINDS THERE ARE PERFECT!"

I EVEN PACKED AN AIR NOMAD KITE WITH OUR STUFF!
WHERE'S THE STRING?
WHY WOULD YOU NEED A STRING?

OH, IT ALL SOUNDS SO *WONDERFUL*, AVATAR AANG!
IT'LL BE MORE THAN WONDERFUL. IT'LL BE THE WAY THINGS *USED* TO BE, IF ONLY FOR A *DAY*.

LOOK, EVERYBODY! WE'RE ALMOST THERE!

WOW!
SHE'S MORE BEAUTIFUL THAN I'D IMAGINED!
HELLO THERE, MR. CRANEFISH! HAPPY YANGCHEN'S FESTIVAL!
WHAT A BEAUTIFUL CREATURE!
KWAAAA! KWAAAA!
BEAUTIFUL BUT NOISY!
THEY'RE PRETTY COMMON AROUND HERE.
HUH. I THOUGHT IT'D BE A STATUE OF YANGCHEN, BUT THIS LADY DOESN'T HAVE AN ARROW ON HER FOREHEAD. WHO IS IT?
TO BE HONEST, I'M NOT SURE.

THE FESTIVAL'S SUPPOSED TO CELEBRATE YANGCHEN'S DEFEAT OF A POWERFUL DARK SPIRIT.
SHE'S THE DARK SPIRIT?
NO...I DON'T THINK SO.

THE AIR NOMAD ELDERS USED TO TELL THE STORY EVERY YEAR, BUT I'D ALWAYS MISS IT BECAUSE I WAS FLYING KITES WITH MONK GYATSO.

YOU'LL HAVE PLENTY OF TIME TO LEARN THE INTRICACIES OF AIR NOMAD HISTORY WHEN YOU'RE OLDER.

ISN'T IT A LITTLE WEIRD TO BE BOWING WHEN YOU'RE NOT SURE WHO IT IS YOU'RE BOWING TO?
WELL... THAT'S JUST WHAT YOU'RE SUPPOSED TO DO FOR THE HOLIDAY.

THAT'S JUST HOW IT'S DONE.

THAT'S JUST HOW IT'S DONE.

BUT WHY DO I HAVE TO BOW TO THAT GIANT SLAB OF ROCK?
YOUNG LADY, THAT'S JUST HOW IT'S DONE.

BUT WHY DO I HAVE TO WEAR THIS SCRATCHY, SCRATCHY DRESS?
YOUNG LADY, THAT'S JUST HOW IT'S DONE.

BUT WHY DO I HAVE TO TAKE SUCH SMALL SIPS?
YOUNG LADY, THAT'S JUST HOW IT'S DONE.

FATHER, I WANNA GO PLAY WITH THOSE KIDS!
I DON'T UNDERSTAND WHY I HAVE TO SPEND EVERY SINGLE DAY LOCKED UP IN THIS HOUSE!
IT GETS SO... SO...LONELY IN HERE.
I'M SORRY, MY DAUGHTER.
BUT THIS IS JUST HOW IT'S DONE.

ALL RIGHT, EVERYBODY! LET'S LINE UP TO DO OUR BOWS!

NO, THANKS.

TOPH, COME ON. DON'T BE LIKE THIS.
I JUST DON'T FEEL COMFORTABLE DOING THAT KIND OF STUFF, ALL RIGHT?
TOPH BEIFONG DOESN'T BOW TO ANYBODY.

BUT THIS IS IMPORTANT TO AANG.
KATARA, IT'S OKAY--
SO IMPORTANT HE DOESN'T EVEN REMEMBER WHO THE GIANT STONE LADY IS? IF IT HASN'T BEEN CELEBRATED IN OVER A HUNDRED YEARS AND THE WORLD DIDN'T END, MAYBE IT ISN'T ALL THAT IMPORTANT AFTER ALL!

HEH HEH! DON'T MIND HER, AIR ACOLYTES! IN FACT, THIS IS A PERFECT LEARNING OPPORTUNITY!

PEACE IS AT THE VERY HEART OF THE AIR NOMAD WAY OF LIFE. WE LET INSULTS FLY PAST US LIKE A GENTLE BREEZE, LEAVING OUR INNER PEACE UNDISTURBED.

COME. THOSE OF US WHO ARE NOT STUBBORN DUNDERHEADS WILL NOW DO OUR BOWS.
HARUMPH! BE MY GUEST!

THAT WAS *INCREDIBLE!*
WOW!
MY GOODNESS!
UM, WERE YOU GUYS DOING SOMETHING ELSE? ALL I DID WAS *BOW.*

DO YOU NEED SOME HELP WITH THAT BACKPACK, JINGBO?
NO, THANK YOU! AS THE MOST JUNIOR AIR ACOLYTE PRESENT, IT'S MY HONOR TO CARRY THE FESTIVAL SUPPLIES!
ACOLYTES, PULL OUT YOUR INSTRUMENTS! IT'S TIME TO WALK DOWN TO THE MEADOW FOR OUR CEREMONIAL MEAL.

HOPE YOU GUYS ARE HUNGRY FOR SOME YUMMY TOFU AND BEAN SPROUTS!
MM!
CAN'T WAIT.

CLANG!
CLANG!

CLANG!
CLANG!

!
KRNK!

IF WE HAVE TO DO THIS, CAN'T WE DO IT QUIETLY?!

TOPH, PLEASE --
I THOUGHT I WAS DONE WITH THESE SORTS OF FUDDY-DUDDY RITUALS WHEN I LEFT GAOLING! CAN SOMEONE AT LEAST EXPLAIN TO ME THE POINT OF IT ALL?!

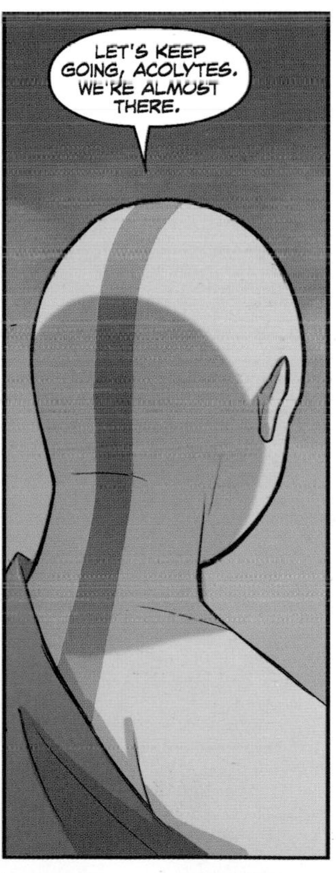
LET'S KEEP GOING, ACOLYTES. WE'RE ALMOST THERE.

AVATAR AANG, IS THE MEADOW JUST BEYOND THAT TOWN?
WHAT TOWN?

OH, NO!
THIS -- THIS
IS WHERE THE
MEADOW USED
TO BE!

NONE OF THIS IS SUPPOSED TO BE HERE. THIS IS... WAS A SACRED PLACE.
A HUNDRED YEARS HAVE PASSED, SWEETIE. A LOT CAN CHANGE.

SNIFF SNIFF SMELLS LIKE...
MEAT!

I'LL ENJOY THE AIR NOMAD CEREMONIAL MEAL A WHOLE LOT MORE ON A FULL STOMACH! WE'LL BE RIGHT BACK!

KATARA? IS THAT YOU?

NIYOK?
I HAVEN'T SEEN YOU SINCE YOU LEFT HOME!
I CAN'T BELIEVE IT! WHAT ARE YOU DOING OUT HERE IN THE EARTH KINGDOM?
泥土火公司
泥土火公司
WE CAME TO WORK AT THAT REFINERY.
"WE"?
NIYOK!
IS THAT NUTHA?
YEP, THAT'S MY SISTER.
NUTHA! IT'S ME, KATARA!

NIYOK! GET BACK OVER HERE!
I SHOULD GO.
WELL... IT WAS GOOD TO SEE YOU...
AANG...?

AVATAR?
WHAT ARE YOU SEEING, AANG?

YANGCHEN JUST APPEARED TO ME AGAIN.
BEHIND THE REFINERY?
YEAH, COME ON!

UGH! WHAT *IS* THAT?!

SMELLS LIKE ROT!

SMELLS ***WORSE*** THAN ROT!

STOMP!

GO AHEAD, GUYS. STEP ON. WE'RE GONNA GO CHECK IT OUT.

BUT DOESN'T THE FENCE MEAN WE'RE NOT SUPPOSED TO BE HERE?
NO. THE *FENCE* ISN'T SUPPOSED TO BE HERE.
MAKE SURE YOU KEEP YOUR KNEES BENT.

STOMP!

HHHOOOOOSH!
WHOOOOM!
WAS THAT FUN OR WHAT?
I LOVE BEING AN AIR ACOLYTE!
UGH. IT'S TEN TIMES WORSE NOW!

THIS MUST BE WHAT YANGCHEN WAS TRYING TO TELL ME. IT WASN'T JUST ABOUT THE FESTIVAL.
THIS LAND WAS ONCE SACRED TO THE AIR NOMADS. NOW IT'S BEING DEFILED.

HEY! YOU'RE NOT ALLOWED BACK HERE! THIS IS PRIVATE PROPERTY!
DON'T YOU PEOPLE KNOW WHAT FENCES ARE FOR?!

SIR, I NEED TO TALK TO WHOEVER'S IN CHARGE OF THE REFINERY.

WHO DO YOU THINK YOU ARE TO MAKE DEMANDS LIKE THAT, KID?
I'M THE AVATAR.

ONCE YOU CROSS THAT FENCE, ALL YOU ARE IS A TRESPASSER.

GUARDS, LET'S GET 'EM OUTTA HERE!

STOMP!
STOMP!
STOMP!
WACK!
WACK!
WACK!
WACK!
SHING!
WHOOOOOSH!

ARE YOU GUYS HURT?
NO, WE'RE OKAY.

MOVE OUT OF THE WAY, AANG! I'VE GOT THEM!
NO! NOT YET!

HERE'S ANOTHER LEARNING OPPORTUNITY!
A LITTLE HELP, PLEASE?

AIR ACOLYTES, AS I TOLD YOU BEFORE, PEACE IS THE VERY CENTER OF AIR NOMAD LIFE.
WE DON'T ENGAGE IN CONFLICT UNLESS ABSOLUTELY NECESSARY.
AARGH!
?!
AND EVEN THEN, THINGS WILL OFTEN WORK THEMSELVES OUT--

--WITH JUST THE SLIGHTEST NUDGE.
BONK!

SEE?
BRAVO, AVATAR AANG!
CLAP! CLAP! CLAP!
THIS HAS GOT TO BE THE BEST FIELD TRIP EVER!

CLAP! CLAP!
FLYING FIRE FERRETS -- THAT WAS AMAZING!

HELLO, AVATAR! MY NAME IS SATORU!

WHAT AN **HONOR** TO MEET YOU! WHAT AN **HONOR!**

U-U-UHH... TH-TH-THANKS?

YOU MUST BE KATARA!

Y-YES!

AND YOU GUYS ARE--?

WE'RE AANG'S STUDENTS, THE ***AIR ACOLYTES!***

NICE TO MEET YOU --

-- BUT WE'LL, *AH,* STICK WITH THE AIR NOMAD TRADITION OF BOWING INSTEAD OF SHAKING HANDS, IF YOU DON'T MIND.

KINDA...I'M THE REFINERY'S ENGINEER, BUT MY UNCLE PUT ME IN CHARGE OF THE ENTIRE OPERATION UNTIL HE AND HIS BUSINESS PARTNER COME BACK.

WHICH IS WHY THE GUARDS SHOULD HAVE CHECKED WITH ME BEFORE THEY ATTACKED YOU LIKE THAT.

WELL, MAYBE YOU AND I CAN SIT DOWN FOR A BIT? I'D LIKE TO TALK TO YOU ABOUT WHERE THIS REFINERY IS LOCATED. THE LAND IT'S BUILT ON --
NO. WAY.

SATORU?
YOU OKAY?

THIS IS THE BEST DAY OF MY LIFE!
PLEASE, SATORU! I'M FLATTERED, BUT YOU'RE MAKING TOO BIG OF A DEAL OUT OF THIS... OUT OF ME! I MEAN, SAVING THE WORLD WAS A TEAM EFFORT! I COULDN'T HAVE --

TOPH BEIFONG!

IT WOULD BE AN HONOR... NO. IT WOULD BE THE EXPERIENCE OF A LIFETIME IF I COULD GIVE YOU A TOUR OF THE EARTHEN FIRE REFINERY!

SATORU, WAS IT?
YOU SAID MY NAME!
SURE, SATORU. LEAD THE WAY.

OKAY IF MY FRIENDS TAG ALONG?
WHAT...? OH, YES! THEM!
OF COURSE YOUR FRIENDS CAN TAG ALONG!

SO GENEROUS OF TOPH TO LET US "TAG ALONG."
NO.
THIS MEAT IS SOOO GOOD. ANYONE WANT A BITE?

I'LL HAVE A BITE.
BY "ANYONE," I MEANT ANYONE VEGETARIAN.

MS. BEIFONG --
TOPH, WELCOME TO THE *EARTHEN FIRE REFINERY!*
NO NEED TO BE SO FORMAL. YOU CAN CALL ME *TOPH.*

YEARS AGO, MY UNCLE DISCOVERED THAT THIS AREA IS PARTICULARLY RICH WITH NATURAL RESOURCES.
BUT HE WASN'T ALLOWED TO DEVELOP IT BECAUSE...WELL... BECAUSE OF *POLITICAL REASONS.*

MY UNCLE ISN'T A VERY POLITICAL GUY, BUT HE *IS* FIRE NATION AND THIS LAND IS *EARTH KINGDOM.*
ACTUALLY, SATORU, THAT'S WHAT I'VE BEEN MEANING TO TALK TO YOU ABOUT.

THIS LAND MAY BE A PART OF THE EARTH KINGDOM CONTINENT, BUT HISTORICALLY THE *AIR NOMADS* HAVE ALWAYS --

AFTER YOU AND YOUR FRIENDS ENDED THE WAR, TOPH, MY UNCLE WAS ABLE TO FIND AN EARTH KINGDOM BUSINESS PARTNER. A COUPLE MONTHS LATER, THEY OPENED THIS PLACE!

WE'RE THE FIRST JOINT BUSINESS VENTURE BETWEEN THE EARTH KINGDOM AND THE FIRE NATION!
BUT, AS I WAS SAYING--

HERE, IT DOESN'T MATTER WHERE YOU'RE FROM, AS LONG AS YOU'RE WILLING TO *WORK HARD.*
SATORU, IF I COULD JUST HAVE A MOMENT--

PEOPLE FROM ALL OVER THE WORLD COME HERE--

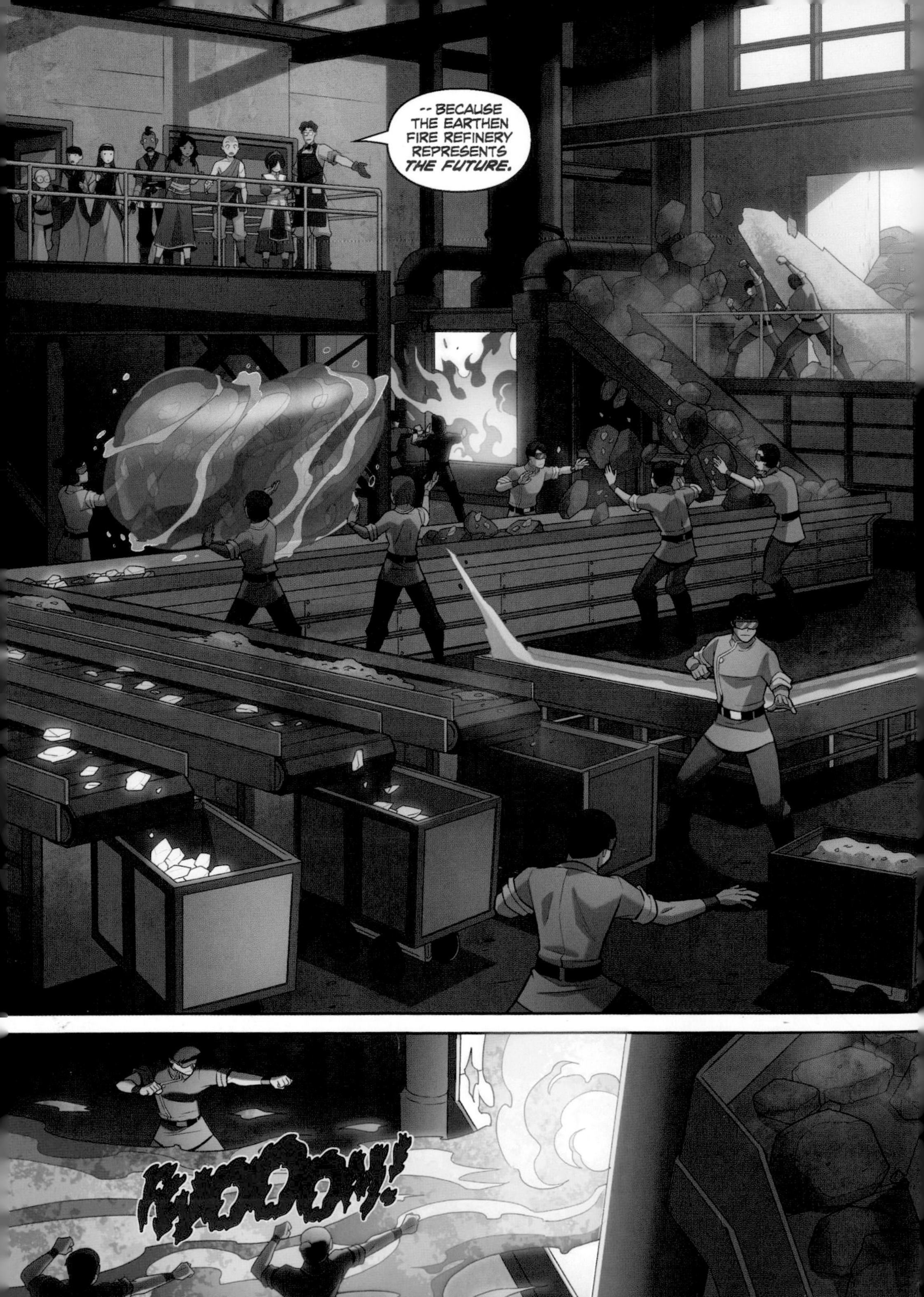
-- BECAUSE THE EARTHEN FIRE REFINERY REPRESENTS *THE FUTURE.*
FWOOOM!

CRUSH!
CRUSH!

WOOOSH!

KCHUCK!
KCHUCK!

WOW.
YOU SAID IT, JINGBO.
IF YOU THINK *THIS* IS IMPRESSIVE, FOLLOW ME.

THAT WAS ACTUALLY OUR FIRST, *OLDER* PRODUCTION LINE.
HERE'S OUR BRAND-NEW ONE, WHICH CAME INTO OPERATION ABOUT A MONTH AGO!
OKAY. MY MIND HAS OFFICIALLY BEEN *BLOWN.*

THIS PRODUCTION LINE DOES THE SAME THING AS THE OLD ONE, ONLY WE'VE REPLACED ALL THE BENDING WITH MACHINES.
I'VE NEVER SEEN SO MANY MACHINES IN ALL MY LIFE! NOT EVEN IN THE MACHINIST'S WORKSHOP AT THE NORTHERN AIR TEMPLE!
WHY WOULD YOU WANT TO REPLACE BENDING WITH MACHINES?

WELL, NOT EVERYBODY'S A BENDER. WITH MACHINES, EVEN NONBENDERS CAN PERFORM TASKS THAT REQUIRE A LOT OF POWER.
POOOM!
POOOM!
POOOM!

PLUS, HOW LONG DOES IT TAKE TO TRAIN A BENDER BEFORE HE'S READY TO WORK FOR US? YEARS?
WE CAN TRAIN AN EMPLOYEE TO USE ONE OF THESE MACHINES IN A COUPLE OF DAYS.
KRAKATA-
KRAKATA-
KRAKATA-

BENDING JUST SEEMS SO MUCH MORE... ELEGANT.

THAT MAY BE TRUE. SO FAR THE BENDER LINE HAS BEEN MORE EFFICIENT.
BUT WE'RE FIGURING OUT WAYS TO IMPROVE THIS NEW LINE EVERY DAY.

WHAT IS *THAT?*

THE FORKLIFT?

RRRRRRR
THAT'S WHAT MOST OF OUR CURRENT OPERATION FOCUSES ON, BUT THERE ARE SO MANY OTHER RESOURCES WE'RE GEARING UP TO EXTRACT!

WE JUST HAVE TO FIGURE OUT HOW TO DO IT. AND WE WILL. LIKE I SAID, THIS IS THE *FUTURE.*
I'M IMPRESSED! THE WHOLE PLACE TICKS AND HUMS LIKE THE INSIDE OF A CLOCK.
RRRRRRRRR

HEY! HOW FAST CAN THIS THING GO?
RRRRRRRRRR
I'M NOT SURE. IT'S NOT REALLY BUILT FOR SPEED. IT'S MORE --

RRRR-- POP!

OOPS. SORRY ABOUT THAT.
NO, IT'S NOT YOUR FAULT. I'M STILL TINKERING WITH THE DESIGN.
FFFSSSS...

HE'S JUST BEING NICE, YOU KNOW. IT IS YOUR FAULT.
I KNOW.
YOU BUILT THIS?
YEAH.

TSK TSK SIGH

I'M REALLY SORRY, BUT I'M GONNA NEED SOME TIME TO GET THIS UP AND RUNNING AGAIN.
I'LL ASK ONE OF THE EMPLOYEES TO FINISH THE TOUR WITH YOU. THEY CAN SHOW YOU THE NEXT BUILDING, WHERE THE CRYSTALS ARE GRADED AND CUT.

STEP ASIDE.

SATORU... THIS ENGINE...

...I CAN *FEEL* IT.

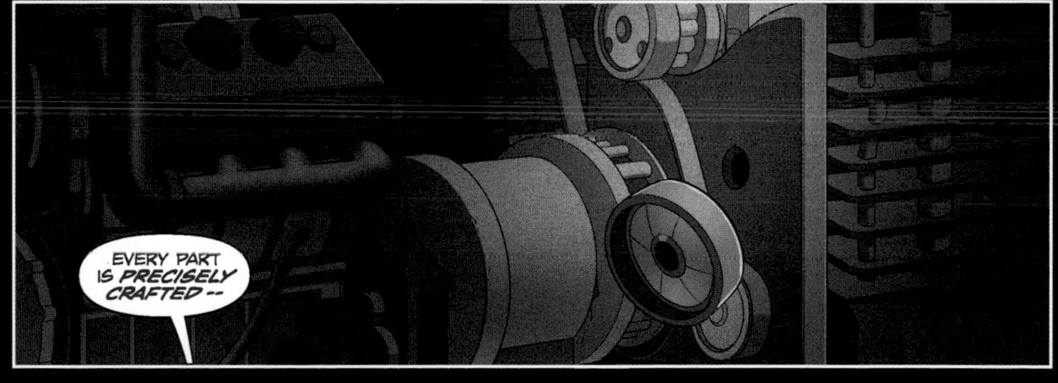

ROARRRRRRR!!

NOBODY BUT *YOU*, YOU MEAN.

RRRRR!

CLANK!

THAT WAS *AMAZING*.

NO SWEAT. EVEN MY MOST NOVICE METALBENDING STUDENTS COULD DO THAT.

YOUR STUDENTS?

I RUN A METALBENDING SCHOOL.

TOPH BEIFONG, IS THERE NO END TO YOUR AMAZINGNESS?

WHAT IF YOU AND YOUR STUDENTS CAME HERE EVERY NOW AND THEN, TO HELP OUT WITH THE MACHINES?
THE BEIFONG METALBENDING ACADEMY ISN'T FAR FROM HERE. WE'RE JUST OUTSIDE OF YU DAO.
THAT'S WHERE MY UNCLE AND HIS BUSINESS PARTNER ARE RIGHT NOW, MEETING WITH THE CITY'S NEW GOVERNMENT! THEY WANT TO BUILD A RAILROAD --
-- TO CONNECT *THERE* TO *HERE.*
OF COURSE, WE'D PAY YOU AND YOUR STUDENTS FOR YOUR TIME.
NO. THEY'RE STUDENTS, NOT EMPLOYEES. BUT YOU *COULD* SPONSOR A NEW SCHOOL BUILDING FOR US.
I THINK MY UNCLE WOULD BE OPEN TO THAT. IT WOULD BE LIKE A...A *PARTNERSHIP* BETWEEN THE REFINERY AND THE SCHOOL.
SATORU, I WOULD *LOVE* TO BE IN A PARTNERSHIP WITH YOU -- I MEAN, THE *REFINERY.*

IS IT JUST ME, OR IS THERE SOME *SERIOUS OOGIE-OSITY* GOING ON OVER THERE?
I THINK IT'S *SWEET!* WE ALMOST NEVER GET TO SEE TOPH'S SOFTER SIDE.

TOPH'S SOFTER SIDE GIVES ME THE *OOGIES.*
AVATAR AANG, IS IT HAPPENING AGAIN?

YANGCHEN, WHAT ARE YOU SHOWING ME? IS THAT WHAT'S HAPPENED ALREADY... OR WHAT'S GOING TO HAPPEN?

ARE YOU ALL RIGHT?
ANYTHING WE CAN DO TO HELP?
I -- I'M *OKAY.* I JUST NEED TO GET HIM TO LISTEN TO ME.

SATORU, I HATE TO INTERRUPT THE, *UM*... *WHATEVER* IT IS THAT'S HAPPENING HERE, BUT I'VE BEEN TRYING TO TELL YOU ALL ALONG --
THERE SHOULDN'T *BE* A REFINERY HERE, LET ALONE A WHOLE *TOWN!*

THIS LAND WAS -- *IS* SACRED TO THE AIR NOMADS! YOU AREN'T SUPPOSED TO BUILD ON SACRED LAND!
AVATAR, I --
NO OFFENSE, TWINKLE TOES, BUT WHAT IS THAT, A RULE FROM THE OLDEN DAYS?

NO ONE'S BEEN HERE FOR A HUNDRED YEARS! IF SATORU AND HIS UNCLE CAN FIGURE OUT A WAY TO MAKE THIS PLACE USEFUL, I SAY GOOD FOR THEM!

BUT YANGCHEN'S BEEN TRYING TO WARN ME... SHE JUST GAVE ME A VISION. I THINK SOMETHING BAD IS GOING TO HAPPEN.
LIKE WHAT?

I'M...I'M NOT SURE...I CAN'T HEAR HER FOR SOME REASON. AND THE VISION WASN'T ALL THAT CLEAR.
HERE WE GO AGAIN! MORE STUFF THAT'S SO IMPORTANT, YOU DON'T EVEN KNOW THE DETAILS!

BUT DON'T YOU SEE? SOMETHING BAD'S ALREADY HAPPENING!
AANG'S RIGHT. JUST LOOK AT THE RIVER! THAT'S NOT WHAT A RIVER SHOULD LOOK LIKE!

ALL RIGHT, EVERYBODY! BACK OFF!

SATORU...

SAY IT AGAIN. ABOUT THE RIVER.

WHAT'S HAPPENING TO THE RIVER --

--ISN'T BECAUSE OF THE REFINERY.

WHAT'S SHE DOING?
TOPH CAN USE HER EARTHBENDING TO FIGURE OUT IF SOMEONE'S LYING.
WOW.

HE'S TELLING THE *TRUTH.*
ALL RIGHT, THEN. I'M WITH TOPH NOW.

MIND IF WE TALK ALONE FOR A MOMENT?

EXCUSE US!

BELIEVE ME, TOPH, I KNOW WHAT IT'S LIKE TO HAVE A CRUSH ON SOMEONE. IT CAN BLIND --

YEESH. SORRY. WHAT I'M TRYING TO SAY IS, SOMETIMES YOU CAN LIKE SOMEBODY SO MUCH THAT IT AFFECTS YOUR PERCEPTION OF THEM.
KIND OF LIKE HOW YOUR PERCEPTION IS AFFECTED BY YOUR FUDDY-DUDDY TRADITIONS?

WHAT --?!
LOOK AROUND, AANG!

PEOPLE FROM ALL OVER THE WORLD ARE HERE, WORKING SIDE BY SIDE! ISN'T THAT EXACTLY WHAT YOU'VE BEEN WANTING FOR YU DAO?

YES, BUT --
SATORU'S RIGHT, THIS PLACE IS THE *FUTURE.*
YOU REALLY WANT TO SACRIFICE THE FUTURE FOR A *STUPID, BACKWARDS HOLIDAY?*

HEY! WHO'RE YOU CALLING STUPID AND BACKWARDS?!
I WAS REFERRING TO THE HOLIDAY, BUT IF THE SHOE FITS --!

?!
RUMBLE! RUMBLE!
?!

WHAT WAS THAT?
I DON'T KNOW.

WHATEVER YOU GUYS ARE ARGUING ABOUT, YOU NEED TO KEEP CALM.
THE WORKERS ARE GETTING SCARED.

WAIT, YOU THINK WE CAUSED THAT EARTHQUAKE?
NONE OF THE EARTHBENDERS IN OUR EMPLOY ARE POWERFUL ENOUGH TO DO THAT.

!!!

!!!

RUMBLE! RUMBLE! RUMBLE!

CRASH!

WHOA. THAT WAS WAY BIGGER THAN THE FIRST ONE!
YOU GUYS OKAY?
YEAH. BUT CAN SOMEBODY GIVE ME A HAND, PLEASE?

TOPH, AVATAR AANG, I'M SORRY, BUT MAYBE YOU GUYS SHOULD LEAVE...
SATORU, AT LEAST LET US HELP YOU CLEAN UP.
NO, JUST GO. PLEASE! MY UNCLE WILL BE BACK AT ANY MOMENT!

CRASH!
POOOM!
POOOM!
ONE OF THE MACHINES HAS GONE CRAZY!
WATCH OUT!
WE NEED TO GET EVERY-ONE OUT OF HERE!
WHOO-SHH!
GO ON! OUT THAT WAY!
SOMEONE'S TRAPPED UNDERNEATH!
HELP ME!
I'LL GET HIM! TOPH --
THERE'S A CORD THAT CONNECTS IT TO ITS POWER SOURCE! YOU NEED TO UNPLUG IT!

--YOU TAKE CARE OF THE MACHINE!
AANG, WATCH OUT!
KRAK!
THANKS!
HURRY!
KROOOOM!
TAKE MY HAND, SIR! YOU'LL BE OKAY!
THANK YOU, THANK YOU!
KRSH!
GOT HIM?
GOT HIM!
POOOM!
POOOM!
POOOM!
POOOM!

SMASH!
THAT WAS DRAMATIC.
YOU KNOW ME.
PLOOP
PLOOP
FFFFSSSS...

TOPH, ABOUT THOSE THINGS I SAID EARLIER --
I KNOW. ME TOO. I GUESS I WAS JUST TRYING TO SAY...
DON'T YOU THINK YOU'RE TRYING A LITTLE TOO HARD TO HOLD ON TO *THE PAST?*

MAYBE. BUT DON'T YOU THINK *YOU'RE* TRYING A LITTLE TOO HARD TO *RUN AWAY* FROM IT?
NOT EVERYBODY'S PAST IS LIKE YOURS, AANG. SOME OF US *HAVE* TO RUN AWAY JUST TO... JUST TO *LIVE.*

AVATAR AANG.
STILL SHOWING UP WHERE YOU'RE NOT WANTED, I SEE.

THE ROUGH RHINOS?! COLONEL MONGKE?! WHAT ARE YOU DOING HERE?

THE OWNERS OF THE EARTHEN FIRE REFINERY HIRED US AS THEIR PERSONAL SECURITY DETAIL, TO PROTECT THEM FROM RABBLE-ROUSERS LIKE YOU!
WHAT'S ALL THIS RUCKUS?! WHO ARE THESE PEOPLE?!
THEY'RE MY GUESTS, AND THEY'RE JUST ABOUT TO LEAVE! UNCLE LOBAN, I CAN EXPLAIN EVERYTHING!

SATORU! YOU CAN START BY EXPLAINING WHAT HAPPENED TO THAT MACHINE THAT COST US TEN THOUSAND BAN!

FFFFSSSS...
PLOOP!

YOU COULDN'T JUST UNPLUG IT?!

WHAT'D I TELL YOU, LAO?! SATORU IS TOO SCATTERBRAINED TO SHOULDER ANY REAL RESPONSIBILITY!
FORGIVE ME, UNCLE! I'LL GET IT ALL SORTED OUT, I PROMISE!
ONE OF US SHOULD HAVE STAYED BEHIND TO MAKE SURE SOMETHING LIKE THIS DIDN'T HAPPEN!
LAO...?
YOU LOOK LIKE YOU'VE SEEN A GHOST.

FATHER.

COMING IN JULY

Toph faces off against her own past in . . .

THE RIFT • PART TWO

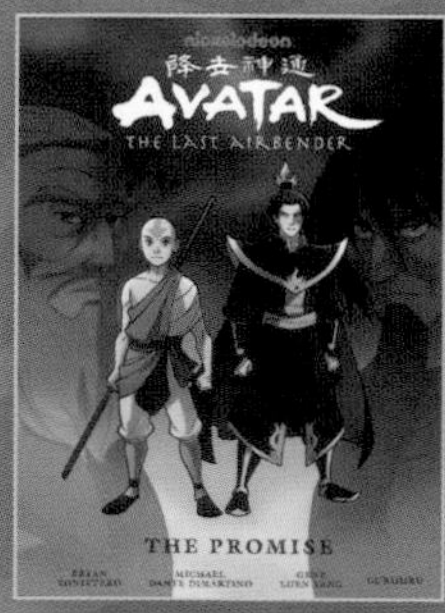

Avatar: The Last Airbender—The Promise Library Edition
978-1-61655-074-5 $39.99

Avatar: The Last Airbender—The Promise Part 1
978-1-59582-811-8 $12.99

Avatar: The Last Airbender—The Promise Part 2
978-1-59582-875-0 $12.99

Avatar: The Last Airbender—The Promise Part 3
978-1-59582-941-2 $12.99

Avatar: The Last Airbender—The Search Library Edition
978-1-61655-226-8 $39.99

Avatar: The Last Airbender—The Search Part 1
978-1-61655-054-7 $12.99

Avatar: The Last Airbender—The Search Part 2
978-1-61655-190-2 $12.99

Avatar: The Last Airbender—The Search Part 3
978-1-61655-184-1 $12.99

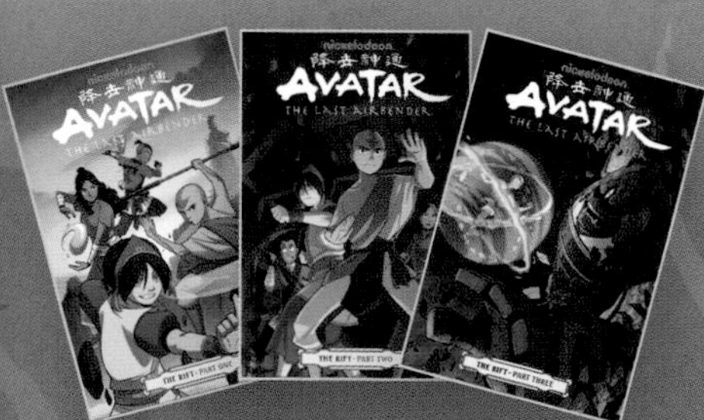

Avatar: The Last Airbender—The Rift Library Edition
978-1-61655-550-4 $39.99

Avatar: The Last Airbender—The Rift Part 1
978-1-61655-295-4 $12.99

Avatar: The Last Airbender—The Rift Part 2
978-1-61655-296-1 $12.99

Avatar: The Last Airbender—The Rift Part 3
978-1-61655-297-8 $10.99

Avatar: The Last Airbender—Smoke and Shadow Library Edition
978-1-50670-013-7 $39.99

Avatar: The Last Airbender—Smoke and Shadow Part 1
978-1-61655-761-4 $12.99

Avatar: The Last Airbender—Smoke and Shadow Part 2
978-1-61655-790-4 $12.99

Avatar: The Last Airbender—Smoke and Shadow Part 3
978-1-61655-838-3 $12.99

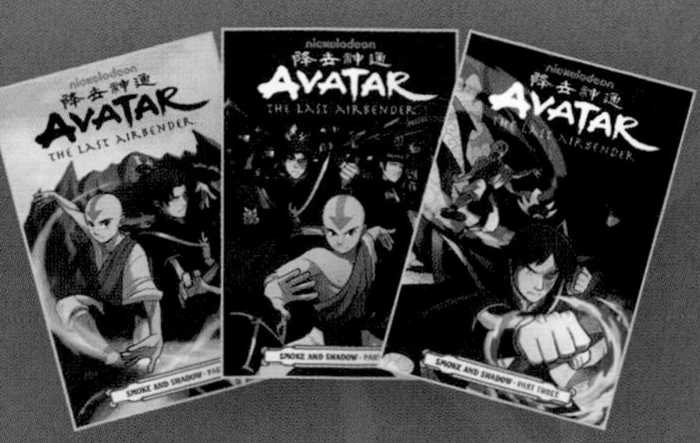